Ready... Set...
CHANGE
AGAIN!

Book design by www.GoodBookDevelopers.com.

Ready... Set... Change
AGAIN!

Take Control of Change
Before it Takes Control of You

Gregg Brown

CONTENTS

Dedication

None of my work on change would've happened without the people that have attended my workshops, speaking engagements, and former coaching clients; the strong people I worked with who were living on the street, living in prison, or working in not-for-profits and corporations; from nurses to CEOs—your names are too many to list—but know you have influenced me in a profound way.

Preface

Early in the start of my career, after some exciting leadership roles, I needed to find deeper meaning in my work. This insight led to me to volunteer and then teach life skills to inmates in medium and maximum security federal penitentiaries. Surprisingly, it was one of the most positive, educational and life-changing events.

I worked with a man we will call Max. Max was about 6 feet, 6 inches tall, a big, burly guy covered in tattoos who you wouldn't want to run into in a back alley! Max was in prison because he'd done some very violent offences and hurt a number of people. He was labeled a dangerous offender, and due to the severity of his sentence could be kept in jail for a very long time. Once I got to know Max I used to joke with him that he was not a white supremacist but a "Max supremacist," meaning if you weren't like Max, he didn't like you and would want to hurt you. We had developed a program of care within the federal penitentiary for inmates to learn how to take care of other elderly and infirm inmates. As part of this three-month program they learned how to make hospital beds, how to do lifts and transfers, how to read to people who couldn't read anymore, as well as alternative forms of care like aromatherapy. The main goal of this program was to teach them empathy and how to interact with people in non-violent ways. Max went through the heavy screening process to enter this program and had been highly engaged in learning all the different pieces of the program. There was no benefit to Max doing this program—he wasn't getting a "get out of jail free" card!

Towards the end of the three-month program, I remember turning around to see Max giving the most tender and gentle foot massage to an elderly black prisoner who could no longer walk. I felt a jolt go off inside me as I thought, "I can't believe what

I'm seeing. If he has changed, we all have this power in us that we don't know we have."

If someone like Max can access this power, use strategies to change his deeply held belief system, then you and I could also use these strategies to make positive changes in our lives. Maybe we can be more open to new ideas, new processes, new habits or behaviours, more open to a new business process or a new way of doing things. If Max can change, we can change, and we can help others change. Working with Max, and the men before him started me on this path of change in myself.

We all have this power in us that we don't know we have.

Let's get started, shall we?

Introduction

Most people don't like to dwell on the past. During one's life, people will experience some form of change whether at work, home, in finance, in one's body as we age, and in many other parts of our lives. There was a time when we had rotary dial phones (if you are old enough to remember!), and now we've evolved to carrying mini-computers, that also happen to be phones, in the palms of our hands. We used to only use desktop computers and over time we have changed and now use laptops and tablets with wireless keyboards! Even in the choice of food we eat, sometimes we just get tired of eating the same old thing; we just want a change. In essence, change encompasses all areas of our lives. Whether you want it or not, change is one factor that occurs spontaneously, continuously—and it consciously and subconsciously affects us as humans. We have to be ready to change. Get set up to change. Then change—and be ready to change AGAIN!

In a world where changes abound, adapting to these changes is something we can't avoid and must deal with. It is just like the weather and how we interact with it. Sometimes the weather changes from hot to cold. We can't say just because we want it to be warm, that we can go ahead to and change the weather—like we would a radio station. It's not possible. What we do instead is find a way to adapt to the weather. One of my mentors once told me that the secret of change is

> *What have you put in place to try to adapt or transform it?*

focusing one's attention on not fighting the old but building the new. This is true because the old is the past and as such nothing can be done to alter it. But what we have in front of us can be managed. A lot of times when I hear people complaining about a situation, I think, "What have you put in place to try to adapt or transform it?" It is very easy for us to complain about a change but many of us don't want to bother with adapting to the change. We live in a world where something that you think is easy to accomplish, might actually be a considered a big mountain to climb for others. Sometimes adapting to the change will then allow you to change the situation.

Furthermore, change doesn't have any kind of preference; it doesn't choose where or when to happen. It doesn't choose to affect only your personal life and leave your professional life alone. If anything, change affects all aspects. Many years ago, I had a job and although the pay wasn't the best, I stayed because I had a great boss! As time went on, my boss was transferred to another area and I ended up working with someone who I didn't get along with easily. I didn't leave because of this new person, because I loved my role. Instead, I began to devise means of actually coping with the new boss. I did every task I was asked to do with care. I showed up with a smile. While other colleagues were discussing how unreasonable my boss was, I continued to persevere to develop a relationship with him. After a period of time, he developed trust in me and would call me for professional advice. When change comes, and it doesn't favour you, devise means of managing and adapting to it—rather than act like it's not occurring. That being said, if something is really bad, and you've tried to adapt, you may need to make a decision to remove yourself from that situation.

If you want growth in any area of your life you need to start by examining a few things. You must start with the thoughts that you think. Your thoughts guide your actions and if your actions are poor, that is generally a result of bad thoughts. It's like making a rash decision without thinking through the consequences. The consequences could be drastic. We've all made decisions like that—and in hindsight we know that they could've been better! So when you consider a change, ask yourself what you are thinking about the situation. If it's not a positive approach, hold off, if you can.

The next line of action is to make a plan. There is hardly anything in life that doesn't require planning. Some plans may take 30 seconds to think through; some may take years. After making a plan, you may want to think of the impact of your plan on others. Our plans never happen in isolation. That's why at work, people don't usually accept our plans without a logical understanding of the impact on others. Once there is an understanding of this—then we get told we are free to start executing the plan.

One of the main ways of dealing with change is to expect it. If you expect change, it doesn't catch you by surprise—as you can anticipate it happening. When we can anticipate change it's much easier to handle—as we want to be able to see the future! If we can't predict what's going to happen, we become uncertain. When what we are seeing matches what we are expecting, on the other hand, we feel more in control and more comfortable handling the change. Before we go deeper into these aspects of change, we need to review the challenges of change so we have an understanding of a variety of elements in which change occurs.

Chapter 1

THE CHALLENGE
OF CHANGE

We need to understand the challenges that can occur and plan for them. The challenges of change present themselves usually with the people in the organization. The reason for this is simply the fact that before change can occur with an organization, it has to start with the people. As we see in nature as evolution occurs, the old way of being tends to be swept away.

Evolutionary changes are unprecedented changes. These types of change occur at work when mergers or acquisitions happen. Just like in nature, the parts we may have enjoyed pre-evolution, are no longer there, and we have to adapt to that—possibly using one of the change processes we mentioned earlier.

In the business world change is a constant factor and you have to adapt to these changes, whether planned or unplanned, as the business environment is constantly changing due to the economy, customer demands, the changing workforce, new technology, and processes.

The challenge of reaching an agreement is always paramount during change. We don't all have the same ideas of how the change should be implemented or planned for—so we must use our influence skills to reach agreement. When a change hasn't been implemented before it can be difficult to see the end result—which is its own challenge in the change process. However, when a change has gone well reproducing the process can be easier than if it has not! Reaching an agreement on the scope of the change in the time constraint is a challenge to making changes in an organizational setting.

Another challenge of change is maintaining standards while changing the status quo. When change occurs it affects how a business operates. It can create a barrier to the new change. The change might be such that it can't work with the previous standards of the business operation, hence there might be a need to upgrade the standards. When one changes standards, it can create double standards and hinder the smooth operation of an organization, and of course, as we know, a decrease in productivity.

The attitude people have towards the change creates challenges as well. One's attitude determines one's behaviours. Embracing change is core to the success of change and if most people in an organization don't embrace the change it will most likely fail. Most of the change models discuss the readiness to accept the change. Consistently modeling the behaviours you want during the change is key. The attitude towards change is integral for the person that initiates the change process, and also for those who have to accept it. If the attitude of a business is putting the customer at the forefront of the change—otherwise known as "consumer friendly" or "customer focused"—it would tend to increase sales as more customers would patronize the business.

One big challenge with change is all the models! Which one to use? Do we use just one for the whole organization? There are many models in the world, and choosing one from all of them isn't easy. When one finally decides on a model; then the question arises: does it fit with the organization and the change we are trying to implement? One size does not fit all! As an example, Elisabeth Kubler-Ross's model wouldn't necessarily be the best fit for a business, where it's been lagging behind in sales, and you want a change process that would increase the sales capability. It is necessary to peruse the business world for a change process that would fit with the particular type of change one wants. One model of change can't be all-encompassing, as change is situational and takes place in the context of one's life and the organization. However, learning about the models can give one an understanding of which one might be most suitable for your change situation.

Of course we can't talk about challenges of change without talking about resistance. As one implements change we know we are going to encounter people that get on board with the change right away; we have individuals who will be in the middle who aren't sure if it's a good idea and not want to engage with the change; and, lastly, we have the 'resistors.' We don't want to spend all our time trying to encourage the resistors, as we really want to focus on the individuals in the

Some people won't agree with your plans.

middle to move them along. But we can't ignore them either! Furthermore, if resistant people are left alone with those who haven't yet decided if the change is good, they can persuade them to their way of thinking. We want to use our influence skills to persuade the individuals that haven't accepted the change, but are not resistors yet! Engaging the resistors in dialogue and listening to their issues is one way to bring them down the change path. Eventually though, one must accept that some people won't agree with your plans, and then the resistant individual needs to make a decision about whether they are going to step into the change or not. Of course, there should be consequences for not engaging in the change.

Consistency is also a major challenge with change. Consistency in this case means a few things. When the change process has been accepted and integrated, maintaining the new standard which the change has brought about is key. We don't want people reverting back to their old ways! Any change has to have minimum standards, systems, and supports in place. The change needs to stand the test of time and not be perceived as a whim.

When change is not maintained consistently, it can affect the organization adversely.

As most people know from personal experience, this is just as important in one's personal life! When you wish to change something about yourself such as a habit, what needs to be done after deciding to change, is that one needs to consistently and diligently maintain the new behaviour, as one can easily revert back to the old way.

When change is not maintained consistently, it can affect the organization adversely. If new standards have been set for customer service, and customers are not being handled in the same way by all the service representatives, the business will definitely receive complaints! This is about the last thing any business person would want for his or her business. Change must be implemented consistently to make progress; otherwise, people will revert back to the old way of doing things.

Uncertainty is also another challenge with change. In David Rock's SCARF model, which is reviewed later in the book, we crave certainty. We want to predict the future. When we initiate change, we expect that it will evolve into a success! But sometimes unforeseen circumstances happen and we can't predict the results, thus uncertainty increases. Dealing with the transitional process of change is one aspect of change that one can't predict. Transition involves dealing with those uncertainties that we go through as we adapt to change. When we are in that 'neutral zone' that William Bridges describes, we face a lot of uncertainty around how the change will impact us and we have many questions that will determine how we adapt to that change. As we manage and adjust our expectations as we go through the change, this helps us prepare for and manage the uncertainties. We can be prepared to be unprepared! Those of us that implement change also face the challenge of managing others' expectations as we go through the change process. Frequent communication about the status of the change helps people manage their uncertainty. Helping people be comfortable with ambiguity and uncertainty is a skill!

Going through the planned stages of change is time-consuming and creates challenges in the workplace as we try to continue our regular day-to-day work, on top of the change. Regardless of which change model you use, they all have a minimum of three stages and each stage takes time to plan and implement. Planning

Helping people be comfortable with ambiguity and uncertainty is a skill!

for change takes time, effort, and usually money. People can lose interest if they don't see some quick wins—or they can get bogged down in the planning process waiting until all the, "'i's are dotted and the 't's crossed." The secret is, once you've got a plan in place, determine the quick wins and get started. One must be agile as we go through the planning process. But don't rush out of the gate without some form of a change plan in place.

Anticipating trends and developing the resulting change initiatives can be a challenge in one's day-to-day work. If an organization doesn't plan for change, the organization becomes reactive, and is constantly responding to external changes and not ones initiated internally. An organization needs to find balance between these two sources of change. Once a plan is in place, the organization also needs to be open to the changes that occur as one starts to implement the plan. The scope, the timelines, budgets, technology, people, and processes may change. We must stay open to these occurrences, and adapt our change plans accordingly. Staying too rigid and forging forward may create chaos and make the plan obsolete if it can't respond to the changing environment. Limiting change to what you plan for would be like steering a ship without trying to fix a big hole that developed in the side of the ship! Eventually, that darn hole would sink the ship! Be open, flexible, and adaptable.

Just wanting to change at work is one thing. However, there is a cost of implementing change and overseeing the change. For each stage of every model, the scope, resources, and costs need to be considered.

Planning for these, determining the appropriate metrics, and applying resources in a structured way will help ensure the change doesn't end up too costly! There is always a cost to change—no matter what anyone says.

While some kinds of changes cannot be predicted, some are predictable and can be planned for. If you work in an organization where there is a usual time of the year when sales are exceptionally low, you can plan for those low seasons and develop strategies to mitigate those low points. Being strategic and planning for these types of changes helps deal with the "ups and downs" of organizational life.

Knowing your core product or service that your organization provides prepares you for changes that may impact it. "Knowing" doesn't mean just identifying it. "Knowing" means understanding its nuances, the intricacies of it, how customers perceive it, how they interact with it, what its strengths and its weaker points are, and what makes your product or service unique. When you know clearly what you provide, the quality level you provide it at, and the costs and timelines attached, you are capable of managing the tradeoffs that occur as you encounter change.

Identifying the major cause and need for change can also be a challenge. Due to the extremely busy nature of most people's work lives, we can sometimes put solutions in place that look to solve a problem, but don't address the actual causes of the problem. Before changes are made, consider and identify what area the changes are impacting and if the change will in fact address the reason for the change. If this is not done it could waste unnecessary resources and time. Most of us don't have time to do "re-work," that is, work that has to be done again. Ensuring we are administering the right change for the right problem will streamline planning efforts and create more successful outcomes.

Finally, as has been said to me many times, don't just change "for change's sake." Examine the models and challenges and determine the best approach and method to manage the challenges.

Chapter 2

WHY WE NEED CHANGE

Change, as we have rightly stated, is a constant factor in life. It is like the air we breathe; it is always happening. Sometimes we notice it and sometimes we don't. Why do we need change when things seem to be going so smoothly? Some of the predominant reasons why we need change include the following:

TO AVOID COMPLACENCY

We all know that to keep our personal relationships alive and well, we have to devote time and energy to

When we have been in our role a long time we can get accustomed to doing things 'the way they've always been done.'

them. If one gets too complacent, our relationships can fade! It's the same for our relationships at work, as well as the work we do. When we have been in our role a long time we can get accustomed to doing things 'the way they've always been done.' Change, whether instigated internally or externally, can encourage us to examine our processes and look for efficiencies or develop a new product or service, or respond to our customers in a different and innovative way. When we undergo change it forces us to view the world differently to knock us out of complacency.

FOR THE PURPOSE OF PROGRESS

Progress in an organization is clearly defined by change. Sometimes you need to reduce your prices to attract the right customer to your line of business. Sometimes you need to change your staffing model to adapt to the type of service you are providing. Doing an environmental scan and understanding what your business needs and drivers are helps to drive progress. Constantly monitoring your organization's and clients' needs and then acting on it, if appropriate, is usually required to stay ahead of the curve.

COMPETITION

In the business world, competition keeps the business going; if one loses track of competition in the business world, you might end up falling behind. In the business environment, sometimes you find yourself at the lower end of a competitive market. It is at this point that you need to realize the need to step it up! Many times, it doesn't have to do with just the quality of the product or service, but who is the targeted audience. When you know your target audience (it could be internal or external clients), you then need to identify the need, the price point, and the quality of what you are providing. Even in a public sector organization competition happens. Whether it's during a procurement process, competing for donation dollars, or applying to the government for funding, non-profit organizations need to look for ways to stand out! Competition can be a good thing, as it can keep us striving for better outcomes. That being said, one can still work in the spirit of collaboration—while staying competitive!

STABILITY

Most people think of change as creating instability. However, when we look at change from what the impact could be, we can see that change could actually ensure stability. In the life of an organization, there comes a time when you need to let go of some ideas and standards to maintain stability. Stability in an organization can't just be bought with money (though stability does usually require investment). Stability in any organization builds trust in the future. Stability builds trust with clients and with the stakeholders. Change and stability work together in an organization to ensure it does not become stagnant. A stable organization can usually undergo larger amounts of change.

INNOVATION

One other major reason why we need change is that it promotes innovation. We can get used to things that are predictable and then fall behind in how we are providing a product or service in our organization.

Getting out of our comfort zone and thinking differently is how innovation happens. Change can create a platform where people can share ideas on new products, processes, technology, and resources. Of course, once new ideas are generated, we need to determine which of those ideas are actually innovative and apply some critical thinking and decision-making skills to determine which ones to implement.

INVESTIGATION

Furthermore, another reason why we need change is that it encourages investigation and questioning. When we investigate and question our existing practices it can help us and our organization grow. We may notice other ideas in our environment, other products, or services that another organization offers, and these may trigger an idea for our business.

STRENGTH

Change makes one stronger. Of course, the more experience one has with a particular change, the easier it is to handle future changes. Whether changes are planned or unplanned, as we adapt to the change, we develop new skills and abilities to handle the change.

Once the change is over, we are at a new level, or as William Bridges says, a "New Beginning." The change might not seem favourable at the outset, but as one goes through it, eventually, we come out the other end. We might not see the benefits for weeks, months or even years in some cases. Of course, if you are in a very negative place about the change, we don't want to hear the benefits too early on, as sometimes we just need to be in the 'negative muck' of the change and deal with that first.

SELF CONFIDENCE

As one develops strength in dealing with change, naturally one's self confidence with handling change will improve. When we have gone through a change, whether positive or negative, and we feel we have handled it successfully, we believe more in our own capabilities to deal with changes in the future. We are motivated to do more. Regardless of the outcome of change, we want to look at what we have learned from the experience, and not focus on how we may have failed. Failing at change is fine, yet our self-confidence will not grow if we stay stuck on the failure. When we shift our focus to what we can learn from the failure, our self-confidence will grow. Self-confidence reassures us and others that we can handle problems that arise, and it promotes our credibility in an organization.

ADAPTABILITY

The more changes one tends to encounter, the more flexible one can become. Of course, if you are encountering too many changes, you may need time to rest and re-charge before you can handle more. Flexibility leads to adaptability. As we become more flexible in our handling of change, we begin to easily adapt to change and realize that

When we shift our focus to what we can learn from the failure, our self-confidence will grow.

change is indeed a major part of life. If we stay too rigid during change, it can be difficult to make effective decisions, as change will often keep coming at us like a wave on the ocean, and if we wait for stability it may never arise. Rigid thinking can stifle innovation. We want to make sure when we make a decision, that the solutions we are proposing actually address the initial issues and aren't the 'same old solutions that we've always done.'

IMPROVEMENT

Improvement is another key reason why we need change. Change will often be driven by the need to improve one's life or business. Most times when people plan the stages of change, it is because they want to improve a product, process, or system in the organization, or improve upon something in their personal life. For instance, the rebranding of an organization is a way of improving how customers view the business. Improvement at a personal level will often arise when we feel deficient in a particular area because of lack of knowledge, and we search for ways to glean that knowledge, whether from classes, the internet, books, or colleagues. We gain the wisdom which has "changed" us in some way.

VALUES EVALUATION

Changes will often force us to reevaluate our core values, whether as a business or who we are personally. At different stages of change we may need to choose what values will continue to guide our business and life practices and what values we may need to let go of. Values drive our actions and behaviours. As we encounter different types of change our values will determine how we handle the change, who we involve in the change, how we will make decisions, and how we will interact with customers or internal clients. Values can shift and change over time; however, we need to be able to clearly articulate those to ourselves, our staff, our clients, and our colleagues.

BREAK THINGS DOWN

Change also helps us realize the need to take things step by step. Many of us tend to think that change happens overnight—and it can! Yet adapting to it and realizing the benefits of the change takes time, whether it's

It takes time for people to adapt to change.

a positive or negative change. When you notice that there is a need to change or transform your organization, the trick is to start small and map out the change in step-by-step increments. Planning then implementing a change process with small, bite-size pieces that lead to more complex ones will ultimately save time, rather than jumping in whole heartedly to a big change. It takes time for people to adapt to change, and we want to layer the changes in, in a way people can understand and incorporate them into their lives. Planning change like this requires us to know what the overall outcome or goal of the change is, then breaking it down into manageable tasks and activities.

PERSEVERANCE

One thing about change that no one can deny is that it requires a whole lot of strength and perseverance to get through it. Sometimes we want to see instant results with change, but unfortunately there is no magic wand. Just because you have a plan, doesn't mean you are going to get the desired result, especially if the change is taking place over a long period of time and has a layer of complexity attached to it. Sometimes things don't happen in the way we like, but this doesn't mean we should relent in our efforts! Most times change is filled with upheavals, and sometimes not a lot of productivity, but if one perseveres and manages it to the end, it does make one stronger. Sounds corny, but it's true!

Tough circumstances make tough people. Tough doesn't mean someone has to be "hard" or "cold"—they can still be nice people! Most people haven't made it to the top (whatever their definition of the 'top' is) without the stress and associated strength that one needs to deal with it. Change is like oil, the crude form of gasoline. It is beneficial, but in its crude form it won't have much value, as it can't easily be used by the masses. But as crude oil is transformed into gasoline it becomes extremely useful to most people! Change on its own or for the sake of change isn't that useful. But as change undergoes the process of transformation and gets incorporated into people's lives, one can begin to benefit from it.

For whatever reasons that we need to change, there are times when we just need to recover from the changes that have happened. When there is a large amount of personal or professional changes happening in your life, it can get overwhelming. Sometimes stepping back and not 'doing' any more changes is what is needed at the moment to allow for some stability and recharging of your energy. This applies to changes we are implementing at work. Allowing people time to incorporate, adapt, and integrate the changes is key; otherwise the changes may not stick, and people may be overwhelmed, and their productivity will suffer.

Chapter 3

CHANGE MODELS

Why One Is Not The Best!

A change is perceived in varying degrees by different people; it naturally follows the principle that no matter how similar our perceptions might be, they can't be the same. Change has a few schools of thought, and these schools of thought all have models attached to them! But before we consider these models it would be essential to define the concept of change. Change, according to the Oxford Advanced Learner's Dictionary, is making or becoming different. Nikos Kazantzakis, a Greek poet, philosopher, and author famous for writing *Zorba the Greek*, and *The Last Temptation of Christ*, was someone who was constantly searching for knowledge and answers to life on this planet. Through his writing and associated experiences he found that, "Since we can't change reality, let us change the eyes we use to see reality." This means that since we can't control or change everyone or everything around us (don't you wish we could!), how we deal with the change must start with us.

The models of change are quite numerous, and none of them have been able to offer an all-encompassing model of how to execute or manage change effectively in both the personal and professional world. Each of them have their benefits and can be used in different change initiatives.

LEWIN'S CHANGE MANAGEMENT MODEL

This model postulates that change is a fundamental part of every business irrespective of its size, industry or age. While organizations that know how to manage change tend to thrive, others that can't manage change will actually fall behind, and this is the reason some organizations, whether private or public, end up not surviving. How successful a business is in managing change will often determine how innovative it is in its field. How management and staff understand the change process and how they model it will make or break this success. Kurt Lewin, back in the 1940s, developed his model which is known as **UNFREEZE, CHANGE AND REFREEZE**, and he refers to these three as the stages of the change process. He explained his model using the analogy of a block of ice. Lewin said, "If you have a cube of ice but realize that what you want is a cone of ice, what do you do? First, you must melt the ice to make it amenable to change (unfreeze). Then you must mold the iced water into the shape you want (change) and then you solidify the new shape (refreeze)."

When we look at change as a process in stages, one can prepare himself for what is coming and also make plans for each stage. If success is going to come from a change, one must start a change process by understanding why the change must take place. Lewin made it expressly known that the motivation for change must be generated before change can occur. This is called the **UNFREEZE** stage. At this point, he suggests examining all the multi-faceted assumptions about one's self and relation with others regarding the change. The unfreezing stage deals mainly with preparing the organization to accept the change that is necessary. In today's terms, we might consider doing an organizational change readiness assessment to determine what we need to do to 'unfreeze' people. The unfreezing stage prepares the organization to understand detailed reasons why the existing way of doing things can't continue. We need to create dissatisfaction with the status quo. It is actually easier at this stage when you have poor financial results, low sales figures, or poor customer satisfaction survey results. With this, it is quite obvious that there is a dire need for change to occur if the organization must continue to operate. This is obviously more difficult if the prevalent attitude is "If it ain't broke, don't fix it." There still has to be a reason to change. To successfully prepare the organization, you might need to start by examining the fundamental aspects of the organization and what beliefs, attitudes, behaviours, or processes need to change.

According to Lewin's theory, the first part of the change process is always the most difficult and stressful. When you start breaking down the way things are done, everything is put off balance and the organization will be in a state of flux. This in itself will often generate strong reactions in people. Without creating the motivation to consider a new plan, a meaningful change will not happen.

The next stage after the unfreezing stage is the **CHANGE** stage where people begin to resolve uncertainties and seek new ways of doing things. Everyone then begins to act in a way that supports the new way of doing things. (I wish it happened that easily!) This process actually takes time, as adapting to the change is not an easy task. To go through this stage people must understand how the change benefits them or will impact them. This is not easy as people have assumptions about how things should be. With this stage people will accept the changes at different times depending on the how they are affected by it—and if they are affected by it in a positive or negative way. Obviously it's easier to accept a change that you see has a positive impact versus one that you perceive as negative. Foreseeing and managing these perceptions is crucial to the Change stage. One of the best options for this approach is communicating and influencing people to accept the change and also let go of the old way of doing things. During this period of change people need frequent and constant communication and reminders. Supports need to be in place to support the new way of doing things along with the accountability if it's not done. This requires caution, time, and effort.

The last stage of Lewin's theory is the **REFREEZE** stage where people have already started embracing the new ways of being! At this stage the organization regains stability. This stage helps to internalize the changes by making sure that the changes are used as the new norm in the course of normal business functioning. It ensures that the changes are properly incorporated and a new stability is reached as the employees feel competent and confident in the work environment and are properly accustomed to the new way of working. In all business dealings change is a constant factor, but the refreezing stage ensures that such change is incorporated and normalized as the new way of doing things. Lewin suggests that if this stage of change is not completed, the next change won't be accepted as people would feel that, "If the last one failed, why would the next one be any different?" We've all heard that at work! In the refreezing stage, when a change process is successful, you celebrate it alongside the employees who managed to stay and adapt through the change. It's a way of reassuring the employees that the next change process could be even more successful.

Lewin's three-stage analysis of change still is relevant. However, today we are in a world of fast-tracking, quick actions, and rapid responses. The three stages will often overlap and are not a simple "start/stop." The unfreezing stage alone in a competitive market economy could kill the business itself, if one took too long at this stage. The plans look promising but slowing down the whole operation may be unreasonable if it reduces organizational output. The change stage is filled with assumptions and, of course, nothing is certain. When the employees begin to feel uncomfortable in their work place they may consider leaving.

Adapting to change takes time and doesn't occur overnight. Having patience and understanding of this process while continuing to implement is essential to adapting to change.

KOTTER'S 8 STEP MODEL

John Kotter, a professor at Harvard University and leading change expert, devised an eight-step change model in his book *Leading Change*, first published in 1995. This model is still relevant today.

The first step of this model is to **CREATE URGENCY**, which speaks to creating the desire for change. If change must occur in an organization, it helps when the entire organization sees the need for it. This creates the motivation to get things moving! It's just not about showing people that the business is in bad shape and there isn't enough revenue. It is of more importance to have an open, honest, and convincing dialogue about what's happening in the marketplace and how it is affecting your ability to compete in said market. In such a conversation you must envision and speak about potential threats to the organization and how this relates to the future. You must examine opportunities that could be exploited and give room for people to air their opinions about the issues you have discussed so far. In addition, you could also talk to customers and stakeholders about any external supports which could strengthen your arguments. Kotter suggests that for change to occur at least 75 percent of the organization's management needs to buy into the change; hence, the need to work on this sense of urgency. He suggests not rushing into the next stage until time has been spent on this step—to prevent future short-term losses.

The second step in Kotter's 8 step model is **TO FORM A POWER COALITION**. This involves visible support from management from key people within the organization. Managing change is not all that change entails; it also involves leading the change. We may think that there are some who were born leaders, yet we also know that others become leaders as they grow. Hence, the leaders in an organization don't necessarily have to be based on hierarchy. People can all be leaders regardless of their job title. To lead the change process, it could start with setting up a team of people who can motivate and propel the change from different parts of the organization, be it through the internal informal network, job position, or strong relationship builders. Once you have a group you need to continue to build urgency and momentum around the need for change. Seeking strong affiliation with those who are the leaders is essential at this stage and to identify the potential challenges of the team is important. The team doesn't have to have everyone from the same department. Having a representation or a fusion of people from different areas that are impacted by the change can't be overly emphasized!

The third step here is to **CREATE A VISION FOR CHANGE**. As soon as people hear about the change people begin to think of how to handle the change, new ideas, and solutions to deal with potential problems. These ideas need to be in tandem with a particular vision that people can agree on. When the vision behind change is shared people begin to understand why you are asking them to do something. When the vision is clear people see what your core goals are and why the directives need to be followed. At this stage there is the need to be selective in the choice of words, as the wrong choice of words could be detrimental to the creation of a successful vision of change.

The fourth step is to **COMMUNICATE THE VISION**, as what you do with your vision after you create it will determine your success. At this very crucial stage change communication will most likely compete with other day-to-day communications and, as such, the vision of change needs to be reiterated in everyday conversations. At this point, communication of the change vision should not only be shared at special meetings but must be emphasized at every possible opportunity during day-to-day operations. There is also the need to use the vision to support solutions and counteract problems; it becomes a part and parcel of the organization's routine, and consequently the change is gradually integrated. It is important to note that there is a need to live the change that you desire from others. If you expect a change from employees in your organization, there is need for such change to start with you and this is best expressed in how you conduct yourself, as we all have heard this: Actions speak louder than words! While it may be necessary to want such change in the organization, it is also very important to carry people along by acknowledging their fears and giving them reassurance that come what may, you will support them the best you can, whether they see the change as positive or negative.

The fifth step is to **REMOVE ALL OBSTACLES**. Obstacles abound during change and there is a prerequisite of removing them for the change to end up being a reality. When the organization gets to this stage Kotter suggests that people begin to talk about benefits to what the change promises. A motivating factor for any form of work is the promise of certain benefits. When people understand that following a particular course brings forward certain benefits they may naturally want to be involved. At this stage of the change process you should begin to consider what resistance is rising against the change. Removing obstacles helps empower the ones that desire the change. As obstacles are removed the change begins to move forward. Not all obstacles can be removed—so you want to focus on the most important ones. At this stage you want to identify (or hire externally) change leaders who will be seen as agents of change. Also, you need to make sure that the organizational structure of your firm, job roles, processes, technology, and other fundamental features of the organization are in tandem with the vision of change. In addition, you must not leave out those who do not

Not all obstacles can be removed—so you want to focus on the most important ones.

understand the whole change process and who are quite resistant to it. If anything, what you need do is to work with them to come to the understanding of why the change is needed. The resistance and barriers to the vision of change must be uncovered quickly so as not to influence the minds of those who have not accepted or are still indifferent about the change.

The sixth step is to **CREATE SHORT TERM WINS**, which involves the practice of celebrating early successes in the change process. If this is not done the critics of the change may jump on the bandwagon and influence negatively the minds of those who have accepted the change! Crucial to this stage is the creation of short-term targets which alongside the long-term goals must be achieved. The team of change agents will most likely have to work exceptionally hard to meet these targets, as the achievement of these small wins tend to motivate other workers to do more and step up to embrace the change. Short-term wins should be visible and shared with everyone. Track and share large and small accomplishments. Money doesn't need to be the driving factor here. Short-term wins that show value in various ways can work! The key here is to reward those who help in the success of this stage.

The seventh step is to **BUILD ON THE CHANGE**. According to Kotter, many change projects fail because victory is declared too early. For change to stick it needs to be able to stand the test of time. Quick wins are only a small part of what needs to be achieved in the long run. All hands need to be on deck and improvements must be effectively made. As you build credibility, identify why the changes have been successful, improve on the success, and try to secure new ways of actually doing more—change systems, processes, procedures in a staged way. In this seventh stage, what needs to be done is to improve on the things that made the change successful so far, and try to set new goals at achieving more. Keep seeking advice and consider new ideas which are achievable and scalable. This will keep the energy going!

The eighth and last step is anchoring the change in the corporate culture in order to **MAKE IT STICK**. The changes need to be integrated into the organizational norms. The corporate culture of a firm determines the actions, and the culture can make or break the vision. The change must be seen in all areas of the organization and if this is done, it will become a part of the organizational norms. The new behaviours that people are doing need to be identified, articulated, and linked up to the organization's success. The company leaders throughout the process must still be seen as supporting and rewarding the new behaviours. Leaders, both formal and informal, have a lot of power in an organization. Losing the support of leaders at this stage would be counterproductive, as you would have to start from scratch again. The change needs to be consistently reiterated, rewarded, and integrated into leadership development, succession planning, and in the development and hiring of employees.

Kotter's change processes are realistic, and if adhered to can facilitate change in the workplace. Yet there are circumstances when you need to react to change without having a plan. And of course, change doesn't always happen in sequence. There is also an assumption, that it only supports a set plan for a particular vision which would last a finite period of time. It is also time consuming! Organizations these days need to be able to follow a process—or at least use this philosophy to lead change. For greatest success,

Kotter's model needs to be strictly followed; if one step is overlooked, it can become detrimental to the implementation of change.

KUBLER-ROSS' FIVE-STAGE MODEL

This model was developed by Elisabeth Kubler-Ross after a large amount of research on the death and dying process. Some people call this model the Grief Model as it talks about various emotional stages that a person has to undergo when such a person realizes that he is near the end of life. In the last 20 or so years, this model has also been used to discuss general changes in life. This model relates more to what a person experiences as one goes through change, rather than focusing on how to implement change. This model helps to deal with the grief and loss that one might experience when having to adapt to change, with the premise being, whether good or bad change, we all will have to deal with the loss of something. For example, if you have just bought your first home, which is a positive experience, you will still experience some losses of leaving your old home. Maybe it's giving up your neighbours, the neighbourhood you lived in, the favourite seating area that overlooked a tranquil view. Those are all losses that you experience, even though you are heading into something even better.

The first of these stages is the stage of **DENIAL**. Denial in this case can be about not accepting or believing the news regarding the change. It could be something negative. This model considers denial as a stimulus effect. When you hear bad news, you then may not want to accept it. Consequently, you may develop an attitude that might be considered defensive—thus being in denial. Whether one agrees or not with the change is not the issue. The fact at this stage is simply that there is a change; you may want to resist it even when you know you eventually have to deal with it. Let's say you are a hardworking and dedicated employee and you've heard a decision has been made that because of 'efficiencies' (and we all know what that means!) your role has been made redundant; consequently, you are now going lose your job. You may not quite believe that's the case, as you've worked evenings, weekends, come in early, provided a very high quality of work, and were someone people looked up to. You'll naturally feel hurt and upset by this news. Most likely you will talk to some other colleagues and express your shock at the news. You just can't quite believe it. That is what Elisabeth Kubler-Ross calls the stage of Denial.

The next stage is the stage of **ANGER**, when the truth begins to get absorbed and you begin to think about the change. Denial converts to anger when one realizes that the change would adversely affect them. It is only at this stage that one begins to blame others for the present predicament, to whom you direct your anger. For example, for someone who just got promoted at work, and now feels he wants to get married—but suddenly loses his job, he may find himself directing the blame to his significant other, rather than examining the work-related reasons.

After anger comes the stage of **BARGAINING**, when you want to get out of the situation, and because of that you look for new means of escaping. Bargaining, in this context, is a defense mechanism to prevent getting worked up by the worst-case scenario and it is a natural reaction to prevent extreme change. Most people have gone through "dating" breakups. Let's say you have been dating the same person for two years and then that person breaks up with you. You may have seen it coming—but it happens. It is at the bargaining stage when you so badly crave company that you seek out another dating partner (the rebound!) to remedy the loneliness, even if it's not the best option for that moment. Work-wise, it happens when you settle for a job that you don't really want, but you think, "It will be better this time."

The next stage is one of **DEPRESSION**, when bargaining is not working. This isn't referring to clinical depression, but a state of mind that we pass through as we adapt to change. Most times, bargaining doesn't work out, as you are acting out of desperation rather than your own positive motivation. At this stage, if you are not careful, you begin to assume that whatever it is you have stepped into won't work out. This can be manifested in the attitude you have towards a change at work. If you feel that a change won't work out it will become noticeable, as what you are thinking will drive your actions. At this stage of depression, you may not 'care' or be bothered about the change. You may feel a little hopeless and 'this is the way it is.' There are many ways to identify this stage: low energy, non-commitment, low motivation, and lack of excitement or happiness. Finding a way to maintain one's positive attitude; talking things out with colleagues or friends and grounding oneself in the realistic facts of the situation are a few ways to move out of this stage. If you stay at this stage, it can become difficult not only for yourself, but for your colleagues, family, and friends.

The last stage of the Kubler-Ross model is **ACCEPTANCE**. This stage tends to occur after a period of time when you realize that there is actually no point in being depressed or fighting the change. Acceptance in this case can come in two forms. The first is resigning yourself to the fact, usually due to frustration. It may look like this: throwing your hands up in the air and saying, "There is nothing I can do; that's the way it is." The second way acceptance may show up is when the person involved tries to motivate herself out of the "bad" change and find something more promising instead. Some people who find themselves in this stage may actually begin to explore options to accept the change. For instance, when someone is let go from her job, she may actually think about another vocation, type of work or company, or additional schooling to further her career.

While this model looks very realistic there are many things that it may not be useful for. Elisabeth Kubler-Ross did focus on the negative side of change and does not look at the idea of change from a positive dimension, which of course makes sense, given she was studying people who were in the death and dying process, or hearing bad health news! One aspect of looking at change with this model is that while it explains change from the perspective of what has happened to an individual, it does not focus on the way forward. Or the way through change. This model is not an explanation for every kind of change or positive change. Yet it is helpful to know the stages, as colleagues can experience even positive change negatively. More importantly, this model can help us be patient and understand ourselves and others when we are experiencing negative change reactions—to know that it's a natural response and eventually we will get out of it.

BRIDGES' TRANSITION MODEL

This model was developed by William Bridges and published in his book *Managing Transitions*. This model focuses on managing the transitions that people go through related to the change and not the change itself. Bridges found that the main reason change initiatives fail, is because the individual's transitions weren't managed. Meaning that they hadn't had the opportunity to focus on how they would adapt to the change. The difference between change and transition highlighted in this model is important to note. Transition, in Bridges's model, is considered the internal process that people go through while adapting to change, while change is something that happens to them, or the external event, whether it is considered positive or negative. Most of the other models follow a set of stages or steps, while this model sees change from the perspective of internal processes or phases that happen to people. Transition occurs as people are experiencing change or going through a change process. Change can be thought of as what is going to happen to the organization. It is often towards the end of a change or the change process that people realize the transitions that have taken

> *Change can also occur very quickly, while transition usually takes a lot more time.*

place throughout the change. Change can also occur very quickly, while transition usually takes a lot more time. It is possible for people to experience change and not feel like they are going through transition. If they haven't experienced the transitions—they will at some point! To best manage the transitions, one must acknowledge the change and note where they are at in the transition phases.

This model focuses on three phases: an Ending, the Neutral Zone and the New Beginning. The first phase—**AN ENDING**—happens when people are exposed to some kind of change whether at work or at home, and they may feel resistance to letting go of what has changed. They may feel the change doesn't need to happen. Even if they do think it's a positive change, one still needs to let go of the things that worked for them in the past. Many times at this phase people may experience fear, anger, denial, or frustration. At this phase, one has to come to terms with the change and be ready to accept that it is happening. As an example, if you get a new job in another organization, you most likely will consider this a positive change. Yet, you will still have to let go of your relationships with your old co-workers, your clients, and the routines you followed. The challenge with this phase for us at work is that we have to consider people's emotions as they experience the end of something. Most of us aren't trained to deal with that, but they must be considered and not glossed over in order for the change to proceed; otherwise, you are more likely to encounter resistance.

The next phase is the **NEUTRAL ZONE**. It's a stage filled with uncertainties, impatience and confusion. It is the phase that bridges the old system or way of being and the new state. This happens once people have decided to accept the change, let go of the old, and adapt to the new state of change. This stage is associated with a lower sense of morale and a higher level of skepticism as people are not certain about the outcome of the new process, but they are participating with the hope that the change will result in something better. Productivity will drop at this stage, as people are using their energy to adapt to the change—to learn the new processes, procedures or technologies, as examples. If you manage this phase well, productivity won't drop too much—and people will be guided through this process with adequate supports. While this phase does have its down sides, it also has its own advantages as you can start to see enhanced creativity and innovation. During this phase there is still a lot of uncertainty, and so new suggestions, inputs, and developments that arise should be talked about, considered, or addressed, while continuing to motivate people.

The last phase is the **NEW BEGINNING**. This phase does not happen immediately! After the neutral zone, the people that were indifferent or having a difficult time adapting to the change, must have been properly guided and given adequate support to get here! When one reaches this phase acceptance becomes crucial, and the energy to make sure that the change process doesn't fail and is sustained becomes vital. During this final phase the change becomes the new norm, and people begin to understand it and its importance to the organization's growth and development. Then, those that embrace the change begin to obtain the required skills to stay with the change and also to reach new goals. People begin to live with the change and start to see the benefits of the change. It is at this point that you begin to see people filled with excitement, and people are more engaged and committed. They may believe that being a part of the change process gives them the understanding of where their part fits into the bigger whole. During this phase, results are expected, and tend to be more visible. People are open to learning and improving.

William Bridge's model of transitions, is a very realistic model of how people experience change. While we may put change management plans in place, the transitions that people have must also be expected, guided, managed and supported. One doesn't need to have a change management plan to experience the transitions. The challenge with this model is thinking through the transitions that the people changing (the change targets) and stakeholders experience, and putting in place the supports to manage those. Due to time pressures, commitments, and financial resources, our energy tends to focus on the change plan and how we are going to implement the change, train the workers, and communicate to people, etcetera. We tend not to feel we have the time or money to get into the change targets' shoes and think through the transitions from their perspective and what they need to know to move through the change. However, Bridges argues, if we don't focus on transitions, the change initiative will most likely fail.

ADKAR MODEL

The ADKAR Model is widely used in today's business world to implement change. This model works from the premise that to drive organizational change, we need to focus on the activities that drive individual change. This model from the outset states that the purpose of change is to achieve a set of goals and each step works towards achieving those goals. Of course there is the business aspect of change. Yet this model, like Bridges's, also focuses on the people side of change. This model looks at specific strategies someone in an organization can use to facilitate people through the change process.

ADKAR is an acronym meaning:

> *Awareness*
> *Design*
> *Knowledge*
> *Ability*
> *Reinforcement*

AWARENESS is the need and requirement of the change; this occurs mainly with changes that are planned. The business reason and how it fits with the larger organizational strategy needs to be understood at this stage. At this stage, what needs to be done is to inform the employees of the need for change and also the requirements for the change to take effect and, of course, be implemented!

The next step after awareness is to create the **DESIRE** to bring about change and be a participant in it. At the Desire stage, we also have to manage the resistance that we will experience, and leaders need to model the behaviours they are asking of their workers.

KNOWLEDGE is how to bring about the change. Change won't fall from the skies (if only it was that easy!). Knowledge is generally acquired through guidance and support such as coaching and training. Knowledge is sometimes acquired through observing others who have undergone these stages before.

At the **ABILITY** stage, we want to determine if people can implement the change at the level that is required. Ability tends to occur after there has been coaching, practice, and time to adapt to the change. At this stage the question becomes, can we put our knowledge about the change into practice? Can we incorporate the change on a daily basis so it becomes a part of our new way of working? We will then know if we are at this stage!

The last stage is **REINFORCEMENT**. Are the systems and supports in place to ensure the change sticks? Are the old systems removed and accountability measures put in place for people to use the new change? Measuring the adoption of change and recognizing the success of the change are key activities to do at this stage.

The ADKAR model is a popular model for many reasons. First off, it's easy to understand. With this model, it is also possible to divide change into different segments and build activities to walk people through the change process and determine where the business change may not be as effective as planned. This model is helpful for both personal and business change. The key with this model, is not to get hung up on the theory, but to look at the activities that need to be put in place to implement the change.

SCARF MODEL

The SCARF model, a more recent model developed by David Rock, takes the view that human behavior underpins successfully adapting to change. David Rock uses brain science and incorporates research from the fields of social, cognitive, and affective neuroscience. He discusses the insights that the brain offers and how it can be applied in the real world. His work is fascinating, as he links physiology with psychology. Rock explores the biological foundations of the way we as humans relate, and has linked it to the theories of the brain, mindfulness, and regulating and managing our emotions, amongst others. What David Rock's research has shown is that when we perceive threats to the five SCARF domains, it is very hard for us to think logically, and manage and adapt to the change. His premise is that these domains must be understood and managed for successful change adoption.

The SCARF model examines the common factors that can activate either a threat or reward response in social situations. Consequently, it then reviews ways to minimize threats and maximize rewards.

The SCARF model entails five major domains:

Status
Certainty
Autonomy
Relatedness
Fairness.

STATUS refers to how we perceive ourselves in relation to others. If we feel our status is threatened, for example, looking slow or incompetent in front of our co-workers, we are more likely not to engage in the change. That is why you see signs on cashiers in grocery stores that say "Please be patient. I'm a trainee." That is an example of managing their status.

CERTAINTY is related to our ability to predict the future. We want to be able to tell people what will stay the same and what will change. People want to see a plan and will also want to have communication back from the plan so they know how things are progressing so they can manage their expectation of the change.

AUTONOMY refers to our perception of how much control we have over events. Giving people choices during change, telling them what they still have control over, will manage this aspect. Also, giving people as much decision-making authority as possible is an option.

RELATEDNESS involves how we connect with a group and develop relationships that are important to us. This can be done through through formal or informal conversations or meetings. Managing the relationships that are important to people and ensuring new team members are incorporated into the team are aspects of this domain.

Last, but not least, is the concept of **FAIRNESS**. Now, fairness does not mean 'equal'; it means equitable. Determining how input will be used, who will be involved, and communicating that is important. Being as open and transparent as you can about processes is key here. How are changes going to be handled and managed on a project? Examples we have seen in the media are ensuring that, during times of economic uncertainty, management isn't seen as getting a salary increase, when there are cutbacks in other divisions.

Understanding the SCARF model helps individuals and change agents maximize rewards and minimize threats during change. The SCARF model helps us to understand why we can't think logically when one of the aspects of SCARF is threatened and how we can get defensive during change. Understanding this model can smooth out conflict, manage people's emotions, help them think rationally, and help people learn ways in which their brain can be used positively during change.

This is one of the best models to understand individual adaptation to change. It promotes the link between our physiology and our psychology and suggests that these aspects need to be managed regardless of what type of change implementation plan is going to be used. If they aren't managed, implementing a change will be difficult and riddled with individual and group conflict.

Chapter 4

WHEN THINGS
GET TOUGH

Shifting Your Response

Sometimes change just feels hard. Sometimes it feels threatening, even before we've experienced it. Yet we can influence our response to the change. Although changing our response is not easy, it is certainly worth a try!

We need to begin by first recognizing the difference between a *true threat* and a *perceived threat*. True threats can be defined as something that poses actual physical harm to you. As we mentioned earlier, in the SCARF model, that trigger often comes from the oldest part of our brain—the lizard brain! Perceived threats, on the other hand, are psychological ones that might never pose true danger to you. The fear of public speaking is one of the most documented fears—yet it truly is not a physical threat to us. I'm not minimizing this fear, just identifying that it's not a truly physical threat.

Once you have learned to differentiate between these two types of threats, you can begin to address the fears by using the following steps:

1. Be open to new possibilities.

The best thing about change is that more often than not it brings something new to your life. Whenever you encounter change you have two avenues open to you: you can be more open to the ideas and experience, or you can be more closed. Just like people at work, they can be more open to your ideas or closed.

2. Feel the fear.

One of the biggest misconceptions that people have about fear is that professionals and experts do not feel it. No matter what you think, what you assume, or what anyone tells you, some things will always produce a response of fear in you. Go into the fear. Unpack it. Determine if it's based on fact or reality. Go into your feelings around it. You may not be able to problem solve yours or other people's fears, but you can acknowledge them -- and that will help move people down the path of change. Ignoring the fear will not work! (For those of you that want to read more on this topic, read "Feel the Fear and Do It Anyway" by Susan Jeffers.)

3. Address your innate response.

Once you are aware of your response to a change, name it, acknowledge it, and address it. We can experience a loss of control as we go through change, so look for ways to be in control of the change that is appropriate—without being a control freak.

Remember though, this is for a perceived threat only! If it's a real threat like a tiger in the forest, it requires a different response. It may mean RUN!

4. See yourself handling the change or perceived threat effectively.

If you have a fear of public speaking you need to close your eyes and see yourself on stage, presenting material effectively with an engaged audience and see them giving you a hearty round of applause afterwards. There have been studies that have shown that practicing something in your mind is nearly as effective as physically doing it! You do need to do both.

5. Practice, practice, and practice some more.

There is no substitution to practice, when adapting to change. You can visualize and see yourself as a successful presenter all you want. Eventually, you have to get up and do some presentations to put your thinking into practice! Whether you are delivering a speech in public, or presenting to a leadership team, the one thing that will guarantee your success and reduce your chances of messing up, is practice. The more you put yourself in a certain situation, the faster you will adapt to it and come up with ways (sometimes subconsciously) to deal with it.

Chapter 5

LEADING DURING CHANGE

Change in an organization is always stressful. Even in situations where change can benefit the organization, it still can be accompanied by a great deal of stress. This stress occurs because individuals need to adapt; which then requires people to use their resources and step out of their comfort zone. A time of change can be made easier by the organizational leaders, managers or executives, or even colleagues. This is a moment in which they should offer plenty of support to their colleagues and employees. But how

> *I believe we are all leaders regardless of our job title, and we all have the ability to shift people's mindset during change.*

should they do this? First off—I don't believe it's about "them" but about us. As I mentioned earlier, I believe we are all leaders regardless of our job title, and we all have the ability to shift people's mindset

during change. Let's take a look at some options to do this:

Model the right behaviours

Social learning theory, proposed by Albert Bandura, suggests that people learn through observation. A person learns when they are exposed to a model and may imitate that model or store the information for later use. Some models are more influential than others. In the case of organizational leaders, it is expected that they will model behaviours related to change. If the managers act nervously or in a negative way, it's likely that others will respond similarly. The leaders have the advantage of being in a role of authority, which makes it likely that people will already be turning to them to see how to react and what is expected. This is an opportunity to teach by example.

Promote openness

An intimidating aspect of change can be the unknown. When people are not sure about how the change will affect them, their role, their job, they might feel more anxious. In a company, especially a big one, rumours may start brewing. Rumours are not usually positive, but negative. This means that it is important to address concerns openly. It is good to give an overview of the planned changes and, if possible, the effects they will have on members of the organization. Sometimes, the changes might not have clear consequences, which is also necessary to address. It is key that employees know their concerns are heard and that the change is being done in an effective way. Honest and adult discussions can help employees feel involved in the process and also can cut down on a lot of unnecessary stress. Even being reassured that they will hear about the impacts as soon as possible (of

Honest and adult discussions can help employees feel involved in the process.

course, a reassurance that is followed through!) can help people feel more comfortable with the change.

Encourage gratitude and kindness

Some changes might have negative consequences, like layoffs or changes in positions. Others might lead to positive consequences on the long-term, but many short-term difficulties, such as working extra hours or lack of vacations and all the accompanying stress. It can be very good for morale to promote kindness and gratitude on an organizational level. Positive psychology, a branch of psychology focused on the study of the positive aspects of human nature with authors such as Martin Seligman, has found that concepts like kindness and gratitude are good for psychological health and well-being. Not a surprise! The organization that promotes it through example and encourages it is likely to have more loyal and motivated members. People who feel welcome at their organization are far more likely to go out of their way to help. Kindness and gratitude, like negativity, can become self-perpetuating cycles. Don't we want kindness and gratitude everywhere? Yes!

In what ways can kindness and gratitude be encouraged during change? It is important to offer fair treatment to employees and be flexible with rules when possible. Be clear and open about how meetings will run. Have a process in place to handle disagreements. Listen to people's concerns (and don't always try to solve them!). Focus on small areas that don't affect the organization significantly. For example, allowing a person to complete his work in the way that works for him. People tend to remember small acts of kindness and respond in kind. Expressing gratitude means acknowledging the contributions and efforts of different employees and recognizing (and rewarding) this effort when possible. Even when a company is changing and not able to offer material rewards, non-material expressions of gratitude can do a lot to boost morale. Be specific about what you are giving thanks for. Create an 'encouragement wall' for people to specifically thank others. Never underestimate the power of words.

> *Kindness and gratitude, like negativity, can become self-perpetuating cycles.*

There are different tools available for leaders who want to offer support when a change is occurring. It is important to find the tools that fit best and focus on setting a good example. The most important thing is to apply these ideas, not just read the words. You can do it!

Chapter 6

COMPASSION, LOSSES, AND GAINS

When confronted with executing change in the workplace, one can be frequently looking at a difficult task. As noted earlier, staff can get confused, angry, distracted, stressed-out, or afraid for their jobs, all of which can bring about decreased performance and lowered morale. How can a leader effectively actualize change while still maintaining employee productivity and motivation?

In order to re-establish productivity, balance, and profitability, leaders require a specific strategy.

Supporting people through change must include techniques along with practical tools that a leader can apply to present or future changes in the workplace.

So, how can you assist workers during change, particularly when you can't slow down, stop what's going on, or give them a chance to get settled at their own pace?

Here are some important approaches to support your colleagues through change:

COMPASSION

Yes, compassion! I know it sounds weird at work, but stay with me. To start with, remember your own reaction when you first heard about the change and were seeking answers concerning the change. If the change impacted you positively, you might have accepted the change—yet most likely you still would've experienced some uncertainty.

If you perceived the change as negative, you may have been anxious, angry, or confused and experienced a range of other emotions your colleagues are currently encountering. It's easy to forget that not everyone has had the time you had to understand the change. You are often discussing the change with your colleagues a couple of days, weeks or months after you first heard it AND after you've dealt with the change yourself. They may be hearing it for the first time.

When you're planning to talk with your co-workers about a change, recalling your initial response can help you be more understanding of their challenges with the change, and to put proper avenues in place to help them adapt to the change. If appropriate, tell them your experiences and remember that not everyone has had the time you have had to process this change.

BE HONEST WITH WHAT PEOPLE ARE LOSING

Before you discuss the change with your colleagues, consider what will specifically change. What would your colleagues say they must relinquish doing, having, or saying? For instance, when you are developing a new process, your co-workers may need to stop simply planning with a couple individuals, or thinking only about their part of the organization. If the new approach is designed to be more strategic and integrated, people will need to build new relationships and learn about other business units. People will have to step out of their comfort zone—the place that is easy and natural to be in. But for most people, when they need to change their behaviour, it's hard; you have to give up something. It could be time, productivity, relationships or any other issue. When you understand this, it will make it easier for you as the change agent to be more patient—and just as importantly, to facilitate that discussion.

WHAT'S NEW?

It's likewise helpful to consider what's new. What do your colleagues need to start doing that they have not done before? For instance, some changes may be procedural: incorporating new stakeholders in a planning meeting. Other changes may require additional skill development or new ways of thinking. If part of a new process includes how that process is going to influence and be used by the entire organization, they may have to learn new skills of collaborative negotiation, influence, and strategic thinking to be effective in implementing the change. This doesn't happen overnight. All of us require time to adapt to the change. Be specific about what will be new. What do you want people to think, feel, behave, and do following the change? If you can't see the end result, no one can!

Chapter 7

EVERY DAY IS A NEW OPPORTUNITY TO LEARN

This book started with a story about positive change with a man in prison named Max. I'll close with lessons I learned about change from working with inmates, as they contain valuable insights for all of us as we go through change.

1. Everyone has a choice.

There are consequences in life from the choices we make. The consequences of illegal actions can lead to jail time, as these prisoners found out! Everyone does have a choice. Be prepared for the consequences of that choice. Your colleague can choose not to get that report completed on time. Your staff member may choose to not show up at work on time. We can't control others; however, we can endeavour to put the pieces in place for them to choose appropriately. Choices=Consequences.

2. Separate the action from the person.

Some of the prisoners were bad people. Period. That being said, I worked with a number of individuals who had done bad things but who had a core of goodness in them—which sometimes took some time to come out! At work, it's very easy to label people and get tied into bad behaviour. When having a coaching or performance discussion, it's essential to separate the person from the behaviour. You learn to do that working with prisoners!

3. People can show up and do their best, regardless of what circumstances are going on around them.

We often have no control over our work environment. Where we work or live is the way it is. However, we can contribute to the environment and either make it a better place, or a worse place to be. Whether they were big or small, young or old, tattooed or not, many inmates I worked with will be in prison for most of their lives. Yet they could make the best of it. Some volunteered at fixing computers, others took care of stray animals, others learned how to care for elderly inmates. It may sound trite, but regardless of your position, if you try to do your best in your role, you can affect change.

4. Changes happen around us that most of us don't have control over.

While we may not be able to control the changes around us, we can control our reaction to them. It's our reaction to the changes around us that determines how we are going to respond. We can get stuck in 'ain't it awful' thinking—and sometimes it is. Eventually, you have to get unstuck and figure out how to work within the system.

5. Always be polite and courteous to others.

Sounds simple right? It's not easy, yet it's one of the most powerful traits as a leader. I noticed while working with prisoners that if you treated them as human beings (albeit who had done bad things), and didn't talk down to them, they were more likely to treat others that way—including their guards! If we treat others with respect and courtesy while going through change—and I do know that's hard sometimes in high-stress work situations –we can have a smoother work life. In prison, it's not easy to be respectful. In our day-to-day lives it's not easy either. However, it's worth a try! If prisoners can do it, we can too!

FURTHER READING

Bandura, Albert. *Self-Efficacy: The Exercise of Control*, 1997.

Barnes, Kim B. *Exercising Influence: A Guide for Making Things Happen at Work, at Home, and in Your Community*, 2015.

Bridges, William. *Transitions: Making Sense of Life's Changes*, 2004.

Bungay Stanier, Michael. *Do More Great Work: Stop the Busywork. Start the Work That Matters*, 2010.

Hiatt, Jeffrey M. *ADKAR: A Model for Change in Business, Government and Our Community*, 2008.

Hoopes, Linda, PhD and Mark Kelly MBA. *Managing Change with Personal Resilience*, 2003.

Jeffers, Susan PhD. *Feel The Fear and Do It Anyway*, 2006.

Kotter, John. *Leading Change*, 2012.

Kubler-Ross, Elisabeth, MD. *On Death and Dying*, 1997.

Laporte, Danielle. *The Fire Starter Sessions: A Soulful + Practical Guide to Creating Success on Your Own Terms*, 2014.

Lewin, Kurt. *The Conceptual Representation and the Measurement of Psychological Forces*, 2013.

Richardson, Cheryl. *The Art of Extreme Self Care*, 2012

Rock, David. *Your Brain at Work: Strategies for Overcoming Distraction, Regaining Focus, and Working Smarter All Day Long*, 2009.

Seligman, Martin. *Learned Optimism*, 2006.

ACKNOWLEDGEMENTS

This book wouldn't have been possible without the guidance, mentorship, and help of the following people: Joy McCarthy, an insightful and wise organizational psychologist; Linda Hoopes, psychologist and founder of Resilience Alliance; Kim Barnes, Janne Rochlin, Eric Beckman and gang at Barnes & Conti; Bryan Vermander who took a chance on me, believed in me and what I could do; the 'best of the best' gang at TidalShift Inc: Sheila Sisley, Lauren Connor, Siobhan Brown, David Donaldson, Catherine McKernan (here it is!); Phil Buckley, change guru extraordinaire; Amy Ruddell (what can I say?); Michael Bungay Stanier (oh wise one); Danielle LaPorte and Michelle Pante who I started the journey with over 15 years ago (the journey continues!); my wise, wise mentor Lois Brummet, words can't express your contribution; Andrew Barker, who showed me all things are possible; Lynda Monk (yes I finally wrote something!); Kirk Fox for freely sharing ideas and insights; psychologist Teal Maedel, whose experience and insights were always there; and Peter Ford for being my sounding board and keeping our lives together throughout this writing journey.

About the Author

Gregg Brown has over 25 years' experience working with individuals, groups and organizations to change behaviours to achieve better results. He has spoken hundreds of times at conferences and events for clients in Canada and the United States. Gregg holds a Master of Science degree from the University of Leicester in the UK with a focus on organizational psychology, leadership and performance and is an Associate Member of the American Psychological Association. He is an avid reader on anything related to psychology and brain science, especially while sitting on his sunny cottage deck overlooking Lake Erie.

Notes